Women of the
WILD WEST

Biography.

Women of the WILD WEST

Katherine Krohn

A&E.

Lerner Publications Company
Minneapolis

For my mother, Betty Stevens Krohn.

The author offers special thanks to: Muffet Brown, great-granddaughter of Maggie Brown; Kristin Iverson, author of Unraveling the Myth: The Story of Molly Brown; *songwriter Nancy Schimmel, for allowing me to quote her song about Annie Oakley; Kristin Johnson at the "New Light on the Donner Party" Website; Michael Ormiston at the Annie Oakley Foundation; Ken Lomax at the Oregon Historical Society; Craig Munger of the Laura Ingalls Wilder Memorial Society; and Paul and Mary Kopco at the Adams Museum in Deadwood, South Dakota.*

This book is available in two bindings:
Library binding by Lerner Publications Company,
  a division of Lerner Publishing Group
Softcover by First Avenue Editions,
  an imprint of Lerner Publishing Group
241 First Avenue North
Minneapolis, MN 55401 U.S.A.

Website address: www.lernerbooks.com

Library of Congress Cataloging-in-Publication Data

Krohn, Katherine E.
    Women of the Wild West / Katherine Krohn.
      p. cm. — (A&E biography)
    Includes bibliographical references and index.
    Summary: Presents an account of frontier life for women in the
American West through the brief biographies of several women,
including Calamity Jane, Molly Brown, Belle Starr, Pearl Hart, Laura
Ingalls Wilder, and Annie Oakley.
    ISBN 0-8225-4980-8 (lib. bdg. : alk. paper)
    ISBN 0-8225-9690-3 (pbk. : alk. paper)
    1. Women pioneers—West (U.S.)—Biography—Juvenile literature.
2. West (U.S.)—Biography—Juvenile literature. 3. Frontier and pioneer
life—West (U.S.)—Juvenile literature. [1. Women—Biography. 2. West (U.S.)
—Biography. 3. Frontier and pioneer life—West (U.S.)] I. Title. II. Series.
F596.K76 2000
920.72'0978—dc21   99-39901

Manufactured in the United States of America
2 3 4 5 6 7 – JR – 06 05 04 03 02 01

CONTENTS

Wearing one of the more "unladylike" costumes of her day, Martha Jane Cannary, better known as Calamity Jane, became a legend in her own time.

Chapter **ONE**

CREATING THE AMERICAN WEST: ADVENTURE AND HARDSHIP

HERE'S **CALAMITY!**" **SOMEBODY YELLED AS MARTHA** Jane Cannary swaggered toward the bar in the saloon. Better known as Calamity Jane, Martha was tall and tough and considered herself as strong as any man. She also liked to have as much fun as any man. Calamity slipped her gun out of the holster at her hip, fired, and *bang,* put a bullet into the ceiling of the tavern. The men all hollered and laughed. The bartender chuckled and handed her a glass of ale.

The female citizens of Deadwood, South Dakota, where Calamity lived for a time, were horrified by her crude, "unfeminine" behavior. But most of the men in town regarded her as a celebrity. One Black Hills pioneer remembered meeting Calamity: "I said, 'Who is that loud-mouthed man' and [somebody] said, 'That ain't no man, that's *Calamity Jane!*'"

Of course, not all the women who settled in the American West were as colorful and well known as Calamity Jane—who perpetuated her own myth by telling tall tales about herself. Nonetheless, Calamity stands as a symbol of the free spirit inside every pioneering woman.

Women of all ages, educational backgrounds, and races settled in the western United States, at a time and place in history referred to as the "Wild West." Most of these adventurous women led simpler (or at least quieter) lives than their notorious and flamboyant western sisters, women like Calamity Jane and Annie Oakley.

Long before the "great migration" of pioneers moved west in the 1800s, women and men were already living on the land. In fact, people were living on the land that became the United States hundreds of years before Europeans arrived in the late 1400s.

Native Americans, the first inhabitants of this land, lived in diverse, complex societies. The native peoples formed hundreds of tribes, spread across North and South America. Each tribe followed its own cultural traditions and spoke its own language. Some groups farmed, while others hunted game for food and furs. Some of the people built homes from animal hides. Other tribes constructed large, apartmentlike villages out of earth.

In the late fifteenth century, European explorers began to visit North and South America in search of riches. They liked what they found in what they called the "New World": a wealth of gold, silver, furs, and "unclaimed" land.

For the next four hundred years, a steady stream of European settlers poured into North and South America. Their arrival in the Americas represented an immense loss—of homelands, cultural identity, and often life itself—for the Native Americans.

THE GREAT FRONTIER

In 1776 the government of the newly formed United States of America established the Appalachian Mountains as a borderline between the Indians and the new citizens, who inhabited the land east of the Appalachians. But this arrangement didn't last long. Using both treaties and violence, the U.S. government pushed the Native Americans farther and farther west.

In 1803 the United States bought the large Louisiana Territory—828,000 square miles of land extending from the Mississippi River to the Rocky Mountains—from France. The Louisiana Purchase doubled the size of the United States. The next year, President Thomas Jefferson appointed Captain Meriwether Lewis and William Clark to lead an expedition up the Missouri River to explore the territory. President Jefferson hoped that the Lewis and Clark Expedition would serve two purposes: to help fur traders connect with Indian tribes in the West, and to find the so-called Northwest Passage, a water passage from the Mississippi River to the Pacific Ocean.

Many Native Americans were helpful in guiding the expedition through the territory. In present-day North Dakota, Mandan and Minitari Indians gave the explorers valuable information about the course of the Missouri River. Later in the journey, a Shoshone woman, Sacagawea, joined the Lewis and Clark Expedition. She was traveling with her husband, a French Canadian fur trader named Toussaint Charbonneau, and their baby. Sacagawea acted as a guide through the difficult terrain. She was also an interpreter and ambassador between the white men and the native tribes, providing invaluable assistance to the expedition.

Although Lewis and Clark did not find a direct waterway to the Pacific Ocean, they learned a lot about the western land and its people, and they made history as the first white men to cross the western half of the United States. Their expedition opened up territories west of the Mississippi River to the citizens of the United States. By 1820 all the land east of the Mississippi was settled, but the land west of the river was still mostly unclaimed by white men and women.

WESTERN MIGRATION

In 1837 the United States faced an economic depression. Banks closed and people lost their jobs. At the same time, troubled easterners heard tales of a western

SACAGAWEA

Sacagawea, born around 1788 in what would later become Idaho, was a member of the Shoshone Indian nation. When she was about ten years old, she was kidnapped by Hidatsa warriors. The Hidatsas sold Sacagawea to a French Canadian trader, Toussaint Charbonneau, who made her his wife.

When explorers Lewis and Clark were traveling along the Missouri River, they met Charbonneau and hired him as an interpreter and guide. Both Charbonneau and his wife accompanied the expedition. Sacagawea proved indispensable, acting as a language interpreter during the journey.

Lewis and Clark meet Sacagawea.

She was familiar with the countryside and proved herself helpful and brave, helping the party get horses, food, and guides.

Some historians believe that the young woman was exploited. She may have been forced to assist with the expedition. Whatever the case, Sacagawea had no way of knowing that the Lewis and Clark Expedition would lead to the destruction of Native American cultures and land.

"paradise," where land was free, farmland was rich, and forests were thick with timber and game. The hope of a more prosperous life drew many easterners west.

Many people traveled west in covered wagons, or "prairie schooners"—horse- or oxen-drawn trailers with a tall, canvas-covered ceiling. Those who could afford the fare traveled west by stagecoach. Others sailed by ship around South America and up the coast to California. By the 1860s, railroads made the westward passage simple, fairly inexpensive, and fast.

As the western United States gradually became settled, the frontier line—the border of the territory claimed by white people—continually moved west, toward the territories along the Pacific Ocean. Territories turned into states. New cities bustled with activity. "Boomtowns," towns that quickly sprang up around mining areas, filled with people.

A Conestoga wagon (named for Conestoga, Pennsylvania, where the wagon was developed) is readied for its journey west.

Robert Lindneaux depicts the forced migration of the Native Americans in his well-known work called The Trail of Tears.

While U.S. citizens built new lives for themselves, Native Americans suffered. In 1830 President Andrew Jackson signed the Indian Removal Act, which gave the government the power to move Native Americans to lands west of the Mississippi River. In the winter of 1838, the U.S. Army marched almost all the members of the Cherokee nation from their homeland in Georgia to Oklahoma. The journey was long and difficult, and food was scarce. About four thousand Cherokees died along the way. This forced trek became known as the Trail of Tears.

The United States continued to expand its territory during the 1840s and 1850s. Texas became the twenty-eighth state in 1845, and in 1846, the United States gained title from Great Britain to the vast and lush Oregon Country. In 1848, after a two-year war, Mexico surrendered the entire Southwest, from Texas to California, to the U.S. government.

In 1848 gold was discovered in California. A year later, more than eighty thousand people headed west, hoping to strike it rich. At first, mostly men traveled to the mining encampments. But as mining areas in California, and later Oregon and South Dakota, prospered, women flocked there too. Some went to join their husbands, while others sought gold, land, husbands, or jobs.

Some women capitalized on "gold fever" by running successful businesses. One miner's wife, Mary Jane Caples, found herself in the baking business. "I concluded to make some pies and see if I could sell them to the miners for their lunches," she said. "I bought fat salt pork and made lard, and my venture was a success. I sold fruit pies for one dollar and a quarter a piece, and mince pies for one dollar and fifty cents. I sometimes made and sold a hundred in a day, and not even a stove to bake them in, but had two small Dutch ovens."

Another miner's wife, Luzena Stanley Wilson, wanted to run a restaurant during the California gold

The discovery of gold in California drew tens of thousands of gold seekers. Everyone hoped to strike it rich, but only a few would.

Some entrepreneurial women took advantage of the gold rush, offering goods and services that reminded prospectors of the comforts of home.

rush. She didn't let the fact that she didn't own a building stop her. She bought some boards and built a table outdoors, under the trees. "I bought provisions at a neighboring store, and when my husband came back at night he found, mid the weird light of the pine torches, twenty miners eating at my table," she recalled. "Each man as he rose put a dollar in my hand and said I might count him as a permanent customer."

Although the gold rush brought riches to a few lucky adventurers, many other disappointed miners didn't find a thing. But people soon had another reason to go west. In 1862 President Abraham Lincoln signed the Homestead Act. This offered any United States citizen 160 acres of western land. The land was free, as long as the settler had the determination and strength to work the land and was willing to stay put for five years.

Between 1840 and 1870, more than three hundred thousand people traveled westward on the overland trails, various routes for traveling *over* the *land*, as opposed to going by sea. Some major routes included the Oregon Trail, the California Trail, the Santa Fe Trail, and the Mormon Trail. Most of the pioneers were men, but thousands of women came too. Many women traveled with their husbands and children. One of every ten female travelers was a single woman. What these travelers had in common was that they went west in search of opportunities and the promise of a better life. Along the way, they encountered new vistas (views) of plains and mountains. They battled diseases, severe weather, and other dangers. They also encountered the native peoples of the land.

Many Native Americans found the "pioneers" strange and disrespectful. The white people thought they owned the land, air, and water, while the Native Americans believed that the land belonged to everyone. A Crow Indian leader named Kangi Wiyaka, or Crow Feather, said, "How can you buy or sell the sky, the warmth of the land? The idea is strange to us. If we do not own the freshness of the air and the sparkle of the water, how can you buy them?"

By 1875 most Native American families were forced to relocate to reservations, areas of land set aside for them by the U.S. government. Many of the people were

Most women, whether traveling with their families or alone, had to adjust to the rigors of life on the trail.

brutally slaughtered as they tried to defend their families and homes. At the same time, the flood of European Americans moving west continued. Between 1877 and 1887, 4.5 million more people came to the West.

By 1890 no more land was available for homesteaders to claim. But for almost two more decades, the spirit of the west remained, in many respects, wild and changing.

Rest stops for the wagon trains did not necessarily mean rest for women, who still had to cook, clean, and mend clothing for the family.

Chapter **TWO**

THE PIONEERS: MAKING A LIFE IN THE WEST

MANY OF THE WOMEN WHO TRAVELED TO AND lived in the early American West preserved their experiences in diaries, travel journals, letters, newspaper articles, interviews, and fiction. For some women, the pioneering experience was an exciting adventure. For others, traveling and making a home in the West was an ordeal, full of hardship and heartache.

VIRGINIA REED: YOUNG SURVIVOR OF THE DONNER PARTY

(1833–1921)

Virginia Reed was thirteen years old in April 1846, when her family began the two-thousand-mile overland trek from their home in Springfield, Illinois,

Like thousands of other Americans, James and Margaret Reed were drawn west by the promise of a better life.

along the Oregon Trail. This path went through Wyoming to the California Trail. The Reed family had packed their covered wagon with as many of their belongings as the vehicle could carry. But they had to leave behind the bulk of their possessions—and their comfortable home—in Illinois.

Several members of the Reed family were traveling together—Virginia, her parents, James and Margaret, and Virginia's ailing grandmother, Grandma Keyes. Virginia's younger brother and sister would ride in another wagon in the thirty-one-person wagon train.

Virginia liked her family's fancy wagon, which she nicknamed the "Pioneer Palace Car." The wagon had a side entrance, like a stagecoach. This side door opened into a cozy space, almost like a small living room.

James Reed was an ambitious man. He had heard about the many opportunities available in the West—the free land and the fast-growing cities. He was excited about the journey and wanted to make it as pleasant as possible for his family. As the owner of a successful furniture factory, Reed could afford to outfit his family's wagon with many comforts. A small stove would keep the wagon's cabin warm, and built-in storage compartments held extra clothes, medicine, food, and dishes. Two high-backed passenger seats, built with springs, would make the long and bumpy ride west more comfortable. There was even a feather bed for Grandma Keyes on the second story of the tall wagon, so the ailing old woman could rest during the journey.

It wasn't easy for Virginia and her family to say good-bye to their loved ones. On the sunny spring morning of their departure, a crowd gathered on the main street of Springfield to bid the wagon party farewell. Virginia tearfully left her schoolmates. Her father shook hands with his many friends, and her mother cried. Grandma Keyes hugged her sons, who had chosen to stay behind.

"At last we were all in the wagons, the drivers cracked their whips, the oxen moved slowly forward and the long journey had begun," remembered Virginia.

About a month after the group left Illinois, the family encountered its first misfortune—Grandma Keyes died. James Reed built a coffin out of cottonwood for his mother-in-law and buried her under an oak tree. He carved the words "Sarah Keyes, Born in Virginia" on a rock as a headstone and placed prairie sod and wildflowers on top of the grave. With this sad task done, the family hurried to catch up to the other wagons in the train.

"We miss her [very] much every time we come into the Wagon we look at her bed for her," wrote Virginia in a letter to a friend.[7]

In July the wagon train reached Fort Laramie, Wyoming, where other wagons joined the party for the journey through the Rocky Mountains. During a stopover in nearby Fort Bridger, the drivers in the party argued about how to make the difficult passage

When a family member or friend died on the trail, folks had to make do and bury the body before continuing the journey.

through the Rockies. Should they take the known, longer trail by way of Fort Hall or a shorter route called the Hastings cut-off? The men disagreed, and the wagon train split into two groups, going separate ways through the Rockies. Virginia's father decided to join the group that was taking the shorter route. This group elected a new leader, a man named George Donner.

The Donner Party was disappointed to find that the Hastings cut-off was virtually nonexistent. There was no trail to follow. To move forward, they had to hack through thick desert scrub. James Reed was worried. His oxen were dying of thirst. Some other drivers planned to search for water for their animals. They offered to take the Reeds' oxen. Soon, however, James Reed was sorry that he had let his animals out of his sight. Tragically, the oxen escaped, leaving the Reeds stranded in the desert. The family no longer had animals to pull their wagon. Other members of the party took pity on the Reeds and gave them four oxen. But the small team wasn't strong enough to pull the heavy "palace" wagon. The Reeds had to abandon their luxurious vehicle and ride in a much smaller wagon.

The Reeds' luck didn't improve. As the trek became more grueling and uncertain, tempers flared among the wagon train members. In October Virginia's father had an argument with a man named John Snyder. The quarrel broke into a fight. Reed stabbed Snyder, and Snyder died.

The Donner Party held a meeting that night to decide how to deal with Reed's act. Because he had been highly respected before the stabbing, and because he killed Snyder in self-defense, the group decided not to punish him by death. Instead, they would banish him from the wagon train. He was instructed to go off on his own toward Sutter's Fort, a U.S. Cavalry base, and seek help for the group, who would soon have to cross the snow-covered peaks of the Sierra Nevada in eastern California. Reed's wife and children would stay with the Donner Party.

With only a horse and a little food, James Reed set out westward, across the desert. In the darkness, he saw something moving toward him. At first he thought it was an animal. But it was Virginia, who had sneaked away from the wagon party. She handed her father a rifle and ammunition, hugged him, and hurried back to the wagon.

While James Reed moved on, the rest of the Donner Party were immobilized, unable to cross the mountains. It was December, and snow was falling steadily. The party was forced to camp on the chilly slopes of the mountains. They found an old log cabin, and Virginia and her mother and a few others crowded in for the long winter. Other families split into groups, built log shelters, and camped nearby.

As the winter wore on, members of the Donner Party did their best to fight off starvation. They were forced to kill their oxen for food. When the meat was gone,

Hoping to survive the long winter in the Rocky Mountains, members of the Donner Party set up camp.

Virginia's mother and the others made soup from the bones that had been thrown away. As time passed, the food supply completely ran out. Panicked, Margaret Reed set off with Virginia into the mountains in search of food, but the freezing cold drove them back to the cabin.

Margaret cut strips of rawhide off the roof of their log shelter and boiled the tough hide into a paste. It tasted terrible, but it kept them alive. She also caught field mice, and she even resorted to killing her pet dog for food. The Donner Party was desperate. People were starving—three people had already died. Some members of the party resorted to a terrible measure. To keep themselves alive, they ate the flesh of those who had died.

Finally, on February 19, 1847, a rescue party from Sutter's Fort arrived, led by Virginia's father, James. "I can not describe the death-like look they all had," he wrote later in his diary. "Bread Bread Bread was the begging of every child and grown person except my wife."

The rescue party helped the Donner Party cross the difficult mountain passage. A month later, Virginia and her family arrived in California.

When Virginia grew up, she lived in California and was a noted equestrian, or horse rider. She married John Murphy, one of the first real-estate developers in California. When her husband died in 1892, Virginia Reed Murphy took over the business, becoming one of the first female real-estate agents in California. Virginia died in 1920.

OVERLAND TALES

While Virginia Reed's overland trip was extremely traumatic, for many women who traveled west, the journey brought new experiences that they remembered fondly. Eliza Hustler, born in Illinois in 1834, made the trip west to Oregon when she was thirteen. Her family arrived in Oregon without any problems, although a baby girl in their wagon train died on the plains.

Later in life, Eliza recalled her childhood journey vividly. "I can still see the plains with the shimmering heat waves, the dark masses of buffalo moving over

A wagon train tries to make its way through thick mud in Echo Canyon, Utah.

the rolling hills . . . ," she told an interviewer, "the campfires of buffalo chips and later sagebrush, the dust cloud hanging over our long train of prairie schooners as oxen, with swinging heads and lolling tongues pressed into the yokes to move the wagons slowly westward to the land of our hearts' desire."

For other women, the overland trip was more trying. While Virginia Reed could ride comfortably in her family's roomy wagon (at least during the first leg of her journey), most women had to walk west, through mud and rock and underbrush, in sun or rain. Families couldn't afford to wear out their animal teams, so anyone who wasn't driving the wagon, including women and children, usually had to walk.

When the wagon train stopped on Sundays for a "rest," women didn't get much hope of that. Mollie

Sanford, who was traveling across the plains in May 1860, wrote in her journal, "We have to roast and bake, and clean up generally, as the men will not stop of week days."

A woman's role on the trail was clearly defined. While the men typically tended the horses and wagons, women were responsible for domestic tasks. They cooked, sewed, cleaned, and cared for their children. Women were also expected to nurse the sick. They used natural remedies such as poke root and willow bark to bring down a fever. Sulfur and molasses were common treatments for stomachache. Trail women used bread mold on wounds and cuts to fight infection.

Women and children were often in charge of collecting firewood or buffalo chips (droppings) to fuel the fire.

A pioneer woman collects buffalo dung in Kansas. Dung was commonly used as fuel.

Accustomed to cooking indoors, some women found it hard to get used to cooking over an open fire—especially when they had to burn smelly buffalo chips.

A female traveler on the Santa Fe Trail remembered her first experience using buffalo chips. "We soon had a large pile of them, & set fire to them, when they immediately blazed up & burned like dry bark, it was laughable to see the boys jump around it," she said, "so, laughing and jokeing we forgot our antipathies to the fire. Some said it had improved all the supper, even the coffee."

Before trail travelers even left home, they were advised to take certain provisions with them. Books like *The Emigrant's Guide to Oregon and California,* published in 1845, gave travelers a helpful list of food items to bring with them, such as 20 pounds of sugar, 200 pounds of flour, 150 pounds of bacon, 10 pounds of coffee, 10 pounds of salt, plus baking soda, vinegar, tea, and dried beans and peas. Dried fruit was also recommended, to prevent scurvy, a disease caused by a deficiency of vitamin C. The trip west wasn't cheap. A sturdy wagon, food, medicines, and other supplies cost between $500 and $1,000.

Some overland travelers were fortunate enough to have chickens and milk cows with them on the journey. But for most migrants, especially as the journey wore on and food supplies ran low, hunting local game was a necessity. Many western travelers killed buffalo, or bison, for food.

Narcissa Whitman, a Christian missionary who migrated west, liked buffalo meat very much—at first. But when the food she brought on the trip ran out and she had nothing to eat but buffalo for two weeks, she grew very tired of it. Whitman also resorted to eating horse meat on the trail. "I do not prefer it, but can eat it very well when we have nothing else," she said.

Travelers had to be resourceful and adapt to the climate and foods of the different regions they passed through. But as strong-willed as they were, the travelers sometimes met problems for which they just

MARCUS AND NARCISSA WHITMAN

Christian missionaries Marcus and Narcissa Whitman were among the first white emigrants to travel the entire length of the Oregon Trail, in 1836. The Whitmans founded a mission among the Cayuse Indians in present-day Washington State. In 1843 Marcus Whitman returned to the East and guided the first large party of settlers to Oregon. Unfortunately, the wagon train brought deadly diseases, such as measles, to the Cayuse population. Since there were no treatments for such diseases at the time, many of the Cayuse people died. The survivors were angry. They blamed Whitman and his cohorts for the deaths. They also resented the missionaries' attempts to make them give up their cultural traditions. In November 1847, the Cayuse massacred Marcus and Narcissa Whitman and twelve other white settlers.

weren't prepared. The most common—and deadly—scourge encountered along the overland trails was disease. Diseases such as scarlet fever, typhus, and measles—all incurable at the time—ran rampant through some wagon trains. These diseases hit the Native American populations even harder, because the Indians had never been exposed to the germs that caused the illnesses, and their bodies could not fight them.

In 1850 a cholera epidemic hit North America. A young Oregon Trail traveler, Abigail Hathaway King, remembered when the fatal illness struck her wagon train. Her six-month-old brother, Hile, died first, near the Cascade Mountains. A woman in the wagon train died too, and Abigail's mother helped bury her. Soon Abigail's mother also got the highly contagious disease.

Abigail remembered, "Father didn't know what to do, so he had her drink a cupful of spirits of camphor. The other people thought it would kill her or cure her. It cured her."

SETTLING IN

At first the West seemed full of promise to many new settlers. But in reality, taming the wilderness was a constant struggle, and working or farming the land was extremely hard work. For women, endless chores and the strain of childbearing made many of them look and feel old before they were forty.

Frontier women often suffered from loneliness. Many families were isolated in the wilderness, with no

Sharing a quilting project helped cut the boredom and loneliness for these pioneer women of Dakota Territory.

neighbors for miles around and their relatives left far behind.

A pioneer on the Rogue River in Oregon kept a journal to ease her loneliness and collect her thoughts. "Alone all day [to] finish a new dress," she wrote. "Wish I had some new book to read to pass [the] time. . . . O! dear, I am tyred of the same dull monotony of time. . . . [I] think if I had the company of some lively female acquaintance I would feel better."

One plainswoman took comfort in a small yellow canary that hung in a dainty cage in the entrance of her sod house, a home dug from the grassy prairie earth. The singing canary was not just a pet but also a small reminder of the life she had left behind on the East

Coast—a reminder of music and art and bright color, things she was starving for in the endless, lonely, grassy plains.

Women who settled in towns were less lonely, but they often craved excitement. An early pioneer born near Salem, Oregon, in 1856, reported, "Because there were fewer things going on, everybody turned out to public affairs, like hangings, or anything of that kind."

WRITER ON THE PRAIRIE: LAURA INGALLS WILDER
(1867–1957)

> Pa said there were too many people in the Big Woods [of Wisconsin] now. Quite often Laura heard the ringing thud of an ax which was not Pa's ax, or the echo of a shot that did not come from his gun. The path that went by the little house had become a road. Almost every day Laura and Mary stopped their playing and stared in surprise at a wagon slowly creaking by on that road.
>
> Wild animals would not stay in a country where there were so many people. Pa did not like to stay, either. He liked a country where the wild animals lived without being afraid.
>
> –from *Little House on the Prairie* by Laura Ingalls Wilder

In 1932, at the age of sixty-five, Laura Ingalls Wilder published her first book, *Little House in the Big Woods*. The novel was a huge success with young readers, and a series of "Little House" books followed. The much-loved books reflect Wilder's experiences as a frontier child, growing up at a time when the midwestern and western United States were still largely wilderness.

She was born Laura Elizabeth Ingalls, in a log cabin in the "Big Woods" of Pepin, Wisconsin, on February 7, 1867. Laura's "Pa," Charles Ingalls, was a farmer, hunter, and skilled carpenter. Caroline Quiner Ingalls, Laura's mother, valued education and saw to it that her children could read from an early age. When Laura was born, she had a two-year-old sister, Mary.

Calling himself a "pioneer man," Pa often followed his urges to move westward. Laura spent her childhood moving from place to place with her family. When she was a baby, her family left Wisconsin and moved to Chariton County, Missouri. But the family didn't stay put for long. Inspired by the Homestead Act of 1862, which offered 160 acres of free land to willing farmers, Ingalls moved his family to the prairies of present-day Kansas in 1869.

But that arrangement didn't last long either. In the fall of 1870, soon after the birth of another girl, Carrie, the Ingallses were forced to leave. The land on which they had built a home had been given to the Osage Indians by the U.S. government. It was now

The Ingalls girls, from left to right, *Carrie, Mary, and Laura, lived a frontier life. Laura would later write of her experiences.*

part of the Osage Diminished Reserve, a reservation. Neighbors told the Ingalls family that soldiers from nearby Fort Gibson and Fort Dodge would soon force any settlers off the land. Meanwhile, the Osage Indians were angry. People like the Ingalls were trespassing on their land. Laura recalled the upsetting time in *Little House on the Prairie:*

> In the middle of the night Laura sat straight up and screamed. Some terrible sound had made cold sweat come out all over her. . . . She screamed: "What is it? What is it?"
>
> She was shaking all over and she felt sick in her middle. She heard the drums pounding and the wild yipping yells and she felt Ma holding her safe. Pa said, "It's the Indian war-cry, Laura."

Before the U.S. Cavalry could force them out, Pa swiftly moved the family back to their home in the Wisconsin woods. There Laura and Mary were happy to attend school in a one-room building called the Barry Corner School.

Still, Pa wasn't satisfied. In 1874 he bought a piece of land near Walnut Grove, Minnesota. There, Pa figured, he could cultivate the wooded area and plow fields for farming. The surrounding area would be full

At home on the range, a family in Nebraska poses in front of their sod dugout. Like the Ingallses, many pioneer families lived in housing such as this.

of wildlife to hunt. The Ingalls family lived in a sod dugout in a creek bank until Pa could build a wooden house. Common on the prairies, dugout or sod houses were crude homes made by digging into a bank of earth. The roof of a sod house was made of sections or strips cut from the grass-covered ground.

Laura and her sisters attended school in nearby Walnut Grove. Laura's favorite subjects were English, history, and poetry. The Ingallses were sure their life was settled in Walnut Grove. Pa grew a bountiful wheat crop, which was sure to bring in good money at the market. But more trouble came:

> There was no wind. . . . but the edge of the cloud came on across the sky faster than wind . . . Plunk! something hit Laura's head and fell to the ground. She looked down and saw the largest grasshopper she had ever seen. . . . The cloud was hailing grasshoppers. The cloud was grasshoppers. Their bodies hid the sun and made darkness. Their thin, large wings gleamed and glittered. The rasping shirring of their wings filled the whole air and they hit the ground and the house with the noise of a hailstorm.
>
> Laura tried to beat them off. Their claws clung to her skin and her dress. They looked at her with bulging eyes, turning their heads this way and that. Mary ran screaming into the house. Grasshoppers covered the ground.

As the grasshoppers moved in on the crops, Laura's mother slammed shut windows and doors in the house, while Pa hitched up the horses. He drove the wagon around the wheat field, pitching hay into tiny piles. Ma came running from the barn with a pitchfork and ignited the hay into small fires. They hoped the smoke would turn away the grasshoppers. Despite their efforts, the plague of insects destroyed the crop.

The Ingallses were crushed. They sat in their house, helpless, while the mass of insects ate their crop. The next year, Pa tried to grow wheat again, but the grasshoppers returned and ate the crop. In November 1875, Ma gave birth to a baby boy, Charles Frederic, called Freddy. The girls were happy to have a baby brother. The next August, the family traveled to eastern Minnesota to help an uncle with harvesting. There, Freddy became ill and died.

When the harvest was over, the grieving Ingalls family picked up their belongings once again and moved farther west, to Burr Oak, Iowa, where Pa's friend owned a hotel. For a while, Laura and her family lived in the hotel, and Ma and Pa helped manage the business. Later the Ingallses rented rooms over a grocery store, and then they moved to a little brick house outside of town. In May 1877, another Ingalls baby, Grace, was born.

Restless and homesick for their friends in Walnut Grove, the Ingallses returned to Minnesota in the summer of 1877. The family lived in town, and Pa supported the family by doing carpentry and odd jobs.

Two years later, tragedy struck again. Mary, at the age of fifteen, had a stroke, which left her blind. The family wanted to send her to a special school for blind people, but they couldn't afford it. Later in the year, Aunt Docia from Wisconsin visited the Ingallses. She had good news. Her husband was a contractor for the Chicago Northwestern railroad company, and he wanted to offer Pa a job as a railroad manager in Dakota Territory. Chicago Northwestern needed smart, strong workers to manage the work crews. When the railroad work ended, Pa filed a claim for 160 acres of free land. The Ingallses were among the first residents of the new town of De Smet, South Dakota.

In 1881 the Ingallses had saved enough money to send Mary to a school for the blind in Vinton, Iowa. Laura wanted to help Mary too. At age fifteen, Laura earned a teaching certificate and was hired to teach at the Bouchie School, about twelve miles from De Smet. Laura was excited to be earning money for the first time. She would be able to help her sister.

Laura boarded with the Bouchie family, who ran the school, but she was terribly homesick. Almanzo Wilder, a twenty-four-year-old local farmer and the brother of one of Laura's former teachers, offered to drive Laura home each weekend to be with her parents. Every weekend, often in harsh weather, Almanzo picked up Laura in his horse and buggy and took her home.

Laura and Almanzo Wilder endured trying times raising a family on the prairie.

During the three years of sitting side by side on the long drive to De Smet, the two fell in love. They married on August 25, 1885. Laura gave birth to a daughter, Rose, on December 5, 1886.

Almanzo and Laura's early years were difficult. Droughts and hail killed their crops. Almanzo got diphtheria, a disease that left him disabled. In August 1889, their second child was born, but he died soon after birth. The family experienced still more misfortune when a kitchen accident burned down their house.

Fortunately, Laura was used to hard times, and she had a resilient, strong spirit. She was also used to moving. For a time, they lived with Almanzo's parents in Spring Valley, Minnesota. Then they moved to Westville, Florida, and in 1892, they headed back to

De Smet. On July 17, 1894, the Wilders left South Dakota for the last time. In Mansfield, Missouri, a town in the Ozark Mountains, they purchased a home they called Rocky Ridge Farm.

In her peaceful later years, Laura began writing. At first she wrote articles for magazines such as the *Missouri Ruralist*. Her daughter Rose, also a writer, encouraged her mother to write down her childhood memories. In 1930 Laura wrote her autobiography, *Pioneer Girl*, but she couldn't find anyone to publish

Laura and Almanzo settled in Mansfield, Missouri. In her sixties, Laura wrote her exciting accounts of growing up on the American frontier.

Laura Ingalls Wilder autographs books for young fans. Her Little House books inspired a very popular 1970s television show.

it. With Rose's help, Laura rewrote the book, creating *Little House in the Big Woods*. The book was an instant success. She went on to write several more books that together became known as the Little House series, including *Little House on the Prairie, On the Banks of Plum Creek,* and *The Long Winter.*

Almanzo died on October 23, 1949. A few years later, on February 10, 1957, Laura died at home at Rocky Ridge Farm. She was ninety years old.

Laura's books continue to charm readers of every generation. They are also a valuable chronicle of life in the United States during the time of western expansion.

Although Laura Ingalls Wilder experienced hard times throughout her childhood, she appreciated her experiences. Everything she lived through as a child on the frontier shaped the person she became. Near the end of her life, in a letter to her readers, Laura wrote, "It is still best to be honest and truthful; to make the most of what we have; to be happy with simple pleasures and to be cheerful and have courage when things go wrong."

Known as "Little Sure Shot," Phoebe Ann Mosey, or Annie
Oakley, hardly ever missed her target.

Chapter **THREE**

LEGENDS: WOMEN WHO MADE THEIR MARK

LITTLE SURE SHOT: ANNIE OAKLEY (PHOEBE ANN MOSEY)

(1860–1926)

> In some far-off country and safely packed away,
> In some dusty attic far from the light of day,
> You'll find a three of diamonds with a hole
>   through every spot,
> And the one who hit that target was Little Sure
>   Shot.
> —"Little Sure Shot" by Nancy Schimmel

Phoebe Ann Mosey was born in a wooden shack in Darke County, Ohio, on August 13, 1860. (Most writers have recorded the family name as "Moses." According to the Annie Oakley Foundation, however, historical records show the name as "Mosey.") Phoebe Ann had thick brown hair and blue-gray eyes.

When Phoebe Ann, or Annie, was born, she had four sisters, Mary Jane, Lydia, Elizabeth, and Sarah Ellen. Soon a brother, John, and two more sisters, Emily and Hulda, joined the Mosey family.

The large family lived on a small farm in the wilderness. The Moseys were very poor. Annie's father was a hunter, and he shot small game with his muzzle loader to feed his family. (A muzzle loader is a gun loaded from the front end with gunpowder, a patch of cotton cloth, and a lead bullet, all tamped down with a ramrod.) Annie liked to play outdoors with her brother and explore the forest near her home.

On February 11, 1866, when Annie was five years old, her father died of pneumonia. Her mother was grief stricken. She was also afraid. How would she support eight children by herself?

As a young child, Annie's brother, John, hunted for small game to help feed the family. Annie usually tagged along and begged her brother to let her shoot. When she was eight, she shot a gun for the first time. "I know we stuffed in enough powder to kill a buffalo," remembered Annie, who downed a rabbit on her first try. But she didn't know that the gun would "kick" (spring back) when it was fired. "I got the rabbit but my nose was broken," she said.

Life just seemed to get harder and harder for the Mosey family. Annie's oldest sister, Mary Jane, contracted tuberculosis, a serious lung disease. At the time, there was no treatment for the disease, and Mary Jane died. Annie's mother sold the family cow to pay the doctor and funeral bills. To support her family, she worked as a midwife, helping women in the area deliver their babies. Before long she met a new man and remarried. Sadly, her new husband died in an accident shortly after the marriage.

Annie's grieving mother was broke and desperate. She couldn't afford to feed all her children. In 1870 she gave her youngest child, Hulda, to a neighbor family. Then ten-year-old Annie had to leave home. Her mother sent her to the Darke County Infirmary, a poor farm—a home for poor, elderly, orphaned, and mentally ill people. In exchange for room and board, Annie was to help with the younger children at the institution. Nancy Edington, the headmistress at the infirmary, was a friend of Annie's mother. Nancy's husband, Samuel, was superintendent of the facility. Annie's mother knew that her daughter would be in good care.

At the infirmary, Nancy Edington took a special liking to Annie. She brought her to live with her own family, in a separate part of the institution. Nancy also taught Annie to sew. Annie quickly became a skilled seamstress. Annie liked the Edingtons, but she missed her home in the country. "I was homesick for

Annie's mother sent her to live at the Darke County Infirmary, above. In the 1800s, it was common for young children to be sent away to work if money was needed at home.

the fairy places," said Annie, "the green moss, the big toadstools, the wild flowers, the bees, the rough grouse, the baby rabbits, the squirrels and the quail."

Within months of Annie's arrival at the infirmary, a local farmer from the nearby town of Greenville came by looking for a girl to help out on his farm. He explained that his wife had just had a baby and needed a helper. Because Annie was good with children, the Edingtons thought she would be perfect for the job.

Annie went to live with the farmer, who turned out to be, in Annie's words, "a wolf in sheep's clothing." He and his wife were cruel to Annie and treated her like a slave.

"I got up at 4 o'clock in the morning, got breakfast, milked the cows, washed dishes, skimmed milk, fed the calves and pigs, pumped water for the cattle, fed the chickens, rocked the baby to sleep, weeded the garden, picked wild blackberries and got dinner," Annie said. "Mother wrote for me to come home. But they would not let me go. I was held prisoner."

Once, while darning (mending holes in clothing),

Annie fell asleep. The farmer's wife was furious and threw Annie outside into the snow. Other times the couple beat her. Annie couldn't bear this situation for long. One spring day in 1872, she ran away. She returned to the Darke County Infirmary.

The Edingtons were glad to see Annie again and wanted to help her. They hired her to work as a seamstress for the infirmary. She sewed attractive collars and embroidered fancy designs on the orphans' drab uniforms. Annie was also placed in charge of the infirmary's dairy. Annie saved the money she earned and waited for better times. "From the time I was nine, I never had a nickel I did not earn for myself," she wrote later.

In 1875, when Annie was fifteen years old, her mother wrote to her and asked her to return home. She had recently remarried and was building a new house. Annie was elated. Finally she would be with her family again.

Before leaving, Annie stopped at the Katzenberger brothers' grocery store on Main Street. Annie had shopped at the store many times for the infirmary. She knew that the Katzenbergers bought fresh game from local hunters. Annie had a business proposition for the men. She explained that she was going to live with her family in the woods in the north. She planned to hunt and trap game, which was plentiful up there. Would they buy the game she sent to town? The Katzenbergers agreed, and Annie was in business.

Annie was a natural markswoman, or gun shooter. She had an almost perfect eye, and she rarely missed a shot. "I don't know how I acquired the skill, but I suppose I was born with it," she said.

Each day Annie headed into the bushy thicket and tall forests near her home. She wore sturdy lace-up boots and knee-length, full-skirted cotton dresses. At first she used her father's one-barrel, muzzle-loading shotgun to hunt. Soon, with her earnings, she bought herself a better gun, a modern rifle that shot lead pellets.

Annie shot and trapped squirrels, rabbits, and other small game. She also hunted birds, such as quail and grouse and wild turkeys. She always hit her targets in the head. That way, she figured, the animals suffered less. Annie had another rule too. "I always preferred taking my shot when the game was on the move," she said. "It gave them a fair chance, and made me quick of eye and hand."

Annie's stepfather, Joseph Shaw, was a mail carrier, and he made two trips a week to Greenville. On those days, Annie packed up the game she had shot, and her stepfather carried it to the Katzenbergers' store. The store owners then shipped the meat to hotels and restaurants in Dayton and Cincinnati.

Diners often praised the meat Annie delivered. They said it tasted better. Because she was careful to hit the game in the head, there was no lead shot (small lead pellets) in the meat.

Annie gave all the money she earned to her mother. "Oh, how my heart leaped with joy," she recalled, "as I handed the money to mother and told her that I had saved enough from my trapped game to pay [the mortgage] off!"

The more Annie hunted, the more skilled she became with her gun. She was thrilled. She was making good money, and she was doing work she loved.

In the 1800s, being able to shoot a gun well was often necessary for survival. People who could shoot expertly were highly respected. After the Civil War (1861–1865), competition shooting became a popular form of entertainment. Skilled shooters could earn a good living by competing with other shooters or exhibiting their expertise.

Annie liked to participate in local turkey shoots. She noticed that she was almost always the only girl in the shooting competitions. Hunting was considered unfeminine, or "man's work," but Annie didn't care. She was proud of her skill. Eventually Annie was barred from the turkey shoots—because she always won.

On a cool, sunny day in November 1875, in Oakley, Ohio, fifteen-year-old Annie Mosey lifted her gun to her side. A friend had recommended that she try her skill against a professional sharpshooter. Annie had never competed against an expert marksman before, but she was ready. She hollered, "Pull!" and the referee released an excited brown pigeon. Annie calmly took aim and fired. *Ka-boom!* She hit the bird. The crowd that had gathered to watch the shooting match applauded and cheered. Annie smiled. Her opponent, Frank Butler, was at a loss for words.

"I almost dropped dead when a little slim girl in short dresses stepped out to the mark with me," Frank said. "I was a beaten man the moment she appeared, for I was taken off guard."

Frank Butler, twenty-four, was a traveling exhibition shooter from the East Coast. He was charming and good humored, with brown hair and a mustache. He was known as a "crack shot," a champion sharp-

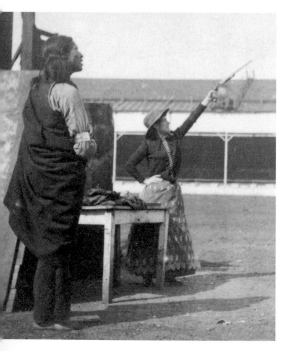

Annie Oakley pitted her shooting skills against some of the area's best sharpshooters.

shooter who had invented several shooting stunts. When he passed through the Oakley area, near Cincinnati, a friend had invited him to compete against an "unknown" local shooter.

"Never did anyone make more impossible shots than did that little girl," Frank said after the match. "She killed 23 and I killed 21. It was her first big match—my first defeat."

Although Butler didn't like to lose, he was impressed. "Right then and there I fell in love with her and I wanted to make her mine," he said.

Before Frank left Cincinnati, he invited Annie to see his vaudeville act at a local theater. Vaudeville was a popular form of entertainment in the late 1800s and early 1900s. Somewhat like a circus, vaudeville consisted of a variety of performances by musicians, singers, champion gun shooters, animal acts, acrobats, comedians, and daredevils.

In his routine, Frank Butler delighted the audience by shooting an apple off his poodle's head. George, the poodle, took an instant liking to Annie. After Frank took his shot, George bowed. Then the talented dog picked up a piece of the shot-apart apple and placed it at Annie's feet.

Soon Frank left town to travel with the Sells Brothers Circus, a popular act of the time. But he couldn't forget about Annie. Frank sent her a letter to say hello, jokingly signing it "George." For Christmas, "George" sent Annie a box of candy.

Deeply in love, Frank set his eye on his target—
Annie Mosey. He sent her a love poem:

> There's a charming little girl
> She's many miles from here.
> She's a loving little fairy
> You'd fall in love to see her.
> Her presence would remind you
> Of an angel in the skies,
> And you bet I love this little girl
> With the rain drops in her eyes.

Within a year, Frank had won the heart of young
Annie Mosey. On August 23, 1876, ten days after Annie's
sixteenth birthday, the well-matched pair married.

For a few years, Annie stayed home while Frank
traveled with his shooting partner, John Graham. In
1882 Annie joined the Graham and Butler act on tour,
but she wasn't part of the show. Then, on May 1 that
year, John Graham became ill and Annie filled in for
him, assisting Frank with his act. Annie held targets
for Frank to shoot. At one point in the show, Annie
held an object that Frank just couldn't shoot. He tried
many times, but he kept missing. The crowd grew
restless. A large man in the audience yelled, "Let the
girl shoot!"

Annie hadn't practiced the shot, but she wasn't going
to be laughed at. She took the gun and fired. She hit
the target! The crowd cheered. Frank again took the

gun, but nobody wanted to see him shoot. The crowd yelled for Annie.

After that day, Annie was the star of the show, and Annie and Frank created their own traveling act. Frank wasn't jealous that people liked Annie so much. He was proud of her.

Annie thought she needed a stage name. Because she and Frank had met in Oakley, Ohio, she decided she would be Annie Oakley. They called their act Butler and Oakley.

Frank taught Annie the stunts he knew. He assisted her while she rehearsed. He threw balls in the air for her to shoot or sat still while she shot an apple off the top of his head. Frank also showed Annie how to entertain an audience—how to build suspense and excitement by making each stunt a little more difficult than the one before it. Frank helped Annie in another way too. He taught her to read and write.

In one famous stunt, Annie shot an apple off a dog's head.

Wearing one of her trademark outfits, Annie posed for a photographer in London in 1887.

Frank suggested that Annie get some nice costumes for her stage shows. Annie didn't like the dresses that were in style at the time—floor-length, hooped skirts and tight corsets. She didn't think that fancy, uncomfortable clothing was practical for a serious gun shooter. So Annie, who was an excellent seamstress, made her own costumes. She sewed leggings and short, full dresses cut just past her knee. She trimmed the dresses with fringe, feathers, ribbon, and ornate embroidery. Most women wore their hair up, fastened securely with hairpins. But Annie's long brown hair cascaded around her shoulders. She liked to wear a wide-brimmed hat that was decorated with a silver star.

Frank and Annie traveled throughout the Midwest by train, performing their shooting act in a variety of theaters. Usually they stayed in cheap hotels. They kept all of their belongings in a trunk, which they hauled with them wherever they went.

Sometimes Butler and Oakley played with other traveling acts, such as the Sells Brothers Circus. In March 1884, they participated in another vaudeville show, the Arlington and Fields Combination.

Besides Annie Oakley, there were a few other noteworthy female gun shooters. Mrs. Ad "Plinky" Topperwein, a well-respected markswoman, traveled the country exhibiting her shooting skills. But unlike Annie, she lacked stage presence and charisma. Lillian Smith was another young shooter with talent— and a tendency to brag about her skills. Tillie Olsen got attention by wearing tights and seductive clothing. But Annie stood apart from the other women in

Lillian Smith (left) *made a name for herself among female shooters in the West. But Annie's talent and charm ensured her a long-lasting reputation.*

her field. She had a quiet charisma and an aura of confidence far larger than her five-foot frame.

Audiences loved Annie's girlish enthusiasm. When she finished her act, she would jump high in the air and click her heels together. "There was magnetism in the way she smiled, curtsied in the footlights, and did that funny little kick as she ran into the wings," said writer Shirl Kasper.

In March 1884, Annie and Frank performed at the Olympic Theater in Saint Paul, Minnesota. One man

In March 1884, Chief Sitting Bull, left, met Annie Oakley in Saint Paul, Minnesota, after one of her performances.

Annie Oakley wears an Indian headdress for a masquerade ball at the Carolina Hotel in Pinehurst, North Carolina.

in the audience particularly loved Annie's act. Chief Sitting Bull was famous for his role in the 1876 Battle of Little Bighorn, in which Plains Indians killed Colonel George Armstrong Custer and his troops. Sitting Bull was deeply moved by Annie's talent—he thought her ability with a gun was supernatural. He was fascinated by her quiet self-assurance. He had never seen a woman like her.

Over time Sitting Bull and Annie became friends. Sitting Bull, who had lost his own daughter a few years earlier, insisted on "adopting" Annie—spiritually—in Sioux custom. This amused her, but she liked him and gladly accepted his offer. Sitting Bull christened Annie *Watanya cicilia,* or "Little Sure Shot."

In 1885 Annie joined Buffalo Bill's Wild West show, an extremely popular outdoor variety show that featured a cast of cowboys and Indians. During the Civil War, Buffalo Bill (William F. Cody) had been a trail scout, Pony Express rider, and buffalo hunter. He was also a hero of the "shoot-em-up" western novels that were popular at the time. He was considered an original frontiersman, "the last of the great scouts." Buffalo Bill called Annie "Missy," a nickname Annie's close friends would call her for the rest of her life.

The performers in Cody's traveling show gave riding, shooting, and roping demonstrations. They reenacted scenes from the wagon-train trail and western dime-novel antics such as Indians chasing stagecoaches.

Annie, billed as "the maid of the Western plains," was the headline act in the show. Frank became her manager and assistant. Annie was not just a great gun shooter, she had become a fine showwoman as well. When she came onstage, she waved and blew kisses. Then, trick by trick, as each stunt grew more complex, she wowed her audience. Annie could shoot with her left hand or right. Sometimes during a performance, Annie stopped shooting and propped her rifle on the dusty ground. With her hand on the barrel, she'd circle the gun for good luck. When she again picked up her gun and nailed her target, the thrilled crowd jumped to their feet, clapping and yelling for more.

Annie could shoot a cigarette out of Frank's mouth, hit a dime thrown in the air, shoot the flames off candles while they rotated on a wheel, and send a hailstorm of bullets through a playing card. Annie's card-shooting trick was so popular that the name "Annie Oakley" became a synonym for a free ticket to the theater. At the time, a complimentary theater pass had a hole punched in it—just like a playing card when Annie was done with it.

Spry and athletic, Annie liked to do handsprings and turn cartwheels. She could shoot targets while standing on a galloping horse or while riding a bicycle. In one stunt, Frank tossed eleven glass balls into the air. In just ten seconds, one by one, Annie shattered each ball. But she saved her best trick for last. Resting her rifle on her shoulder, she turned her back to her target. Then looking at the target with the shiny blade of her pocketknife, she took aim and fired. She never missed!

Buffalo Bill's Wild West show played in over one hundred cities in a year. The troupe traveled all over Europe, Asia, and North and South America. Annie showed off her amazing abilities to world leaders in many countries. For a few years, Annie Oakley was the most famous woman in the world.

In Germany Annie performed her cigarette trick with Kaiser Wilhelm, the crown prince of Germany. The prince lit a cigarette and placed it in a cigarette holder. From thirty feet away, Annie took aim and

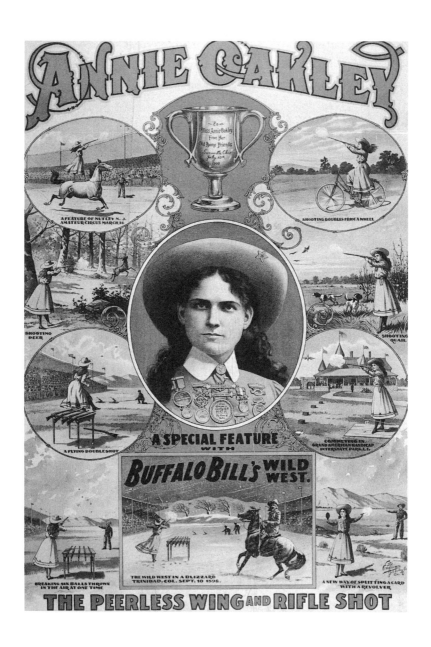

shot the cigarette out of his mouth. The king of Senegal saw the act in Paris and was so taken with Annie that he tried to buy her. He offered Buffalo Bill 100,000 francs for her. Annie was amused, but she politely informed the king that she was not for sale.

As an adult, Annie never forgot her difficult childhood years. She found ways to help needy children, such as talking Buffalo Bill into offering a weekly Orphan Day. On that day, kids without parents got free tickets to the show, and they were treated to candy and ice cream cones.

In 1901 a train carrying the Wild West performers crashed in North Carolina. The accident left Annie partially paralyzed, ending her sixteen-year career with the Wild West show.

Unable to work, Annie was forced to make some major adjustments in her life. She and Frank bought a house in New Jersey. For the first time in their married life, they weren't on the road. Over time Annie had grown accustomed to living in a tent and keeping all of her belongings in a trunk. Even though she now had a big house, she couldn't bring herself to keep her clothes in a closet. She still stored her belongings in a trunk, as she had done for so many years.

Buffalo Bill's Wild West show advertised Annie, "the peerless wing and rifle shot," on some of its posters, facing page.

Annie, in black hat with gun, *gave shooting lessons to many women in the early 1900s.*

Eventually Annie recovered from the accident. In 1912 she was happy to tour one final time, in a show called the Young Buffalo Wild West.

In her later years, Annie kept busy shooting in local competitions and teaching women how to use guns. Annie gave free shooting lessons to more than two thousand women. She trained more than fifteen thousand women in firearm safety and marksmanship. She also gave benefit shooting performances. All proceeds went to children's charities and to young women who wanted to pursue a college education. Annie helped over twenty women attend college.

On November 3, 1926, in Greenville, Ohio, Annie Oakley died after a short illness. Just a few weeks later, Frank Butler followed his beloved wife.

Throughout her life, Annie Oakley reached out to help those in need. She cared about people, especially children. Annie made one final act of generosity shortly before her death. She had her many silver and gold medals melted down and gave the money they earned to a children's charity.

THE UNSINKABLE MOLLY BROWN: MARGARET TOBIN BROWN

(1867–1932)

Margaret Tobin Brown sat in her plush cabin at the forward end of the B deck on the vast luxury ship the *Titanic*. It was about 11:00 P.M. on April 14, 1912. Maggie couldn't sleep. She was reading a book and munching on crackers.

Throughout her life, Margaret Tobin Brown's close friends and family called her Maggie. After her death-defying experience on the Titanic, *Maggie was portrayed on stage and screen as the "Unsinkable Molly Brown."*

Maggie felt fortunate to have an electric heater in her room. Unlike the second- and third-class cabins, the cozy first-class cabin was shielded from the frigid sea air.

Four days earlier, Maggie, a stately, well-dressed woman of forty-four, had boarded the *Titanic* in Southampton, England. She had been touring Europe and was heading to New York. From there she would take a train to Kansas City, Missouri, to see her first grandchild, Lawrence Jr. The baby boy was ill, and Maggie was concerned. She was glad to be aboard the swift ocean liner—she would be in New York in two days. After the visit with her family in Kansas City, she planned to conclude her travels and return to her home in Denver, Colorado.

Unlike most of her fellow first-class passengers, Maggie did not begin life in a wealthy family. Margaret Tobin was born on July 18, 1867, in the small town of Hannibal, Missouri. Her parents, John Tobin and Johanna Collins Tobin, were poor, hard-working, Irish immigrants who met in Hannibal.

Both John and Johanna were widowed when they met, and each had a child. John had a daughter named Catherine, who was eleven. Johanna also had a daughter, ten-year-old Mary Ann. The couple had their first child together, Daniel, in 1863. Four years later, Maggie was born. Two years later, another boy, William, joined the family, and a sister, Ellen (called Helen), was born when Maggie was six.

Maggie's childhood home, above, *had just three rooms—a bedroom, a kitchen, and a front room.*

Maggie and her brothers and sisters attended school in the home of their aunt, Mary O'Leary. Maggie's father labored at the Hannibal Gas Works to support his large family, but the Tobins still struggled to pay their bills. In 1880, when Maggie was thirteen, she completed her studies and was expected to get a job to help feed the family.

Maggie found work at Garth's Tobacco Factory, stripping leaves off tobacco plants at harvesttime. She didn't mind working, but she yearned for a better life. Her half sister, Mary Ann, had married and moved to Leadville, a mining town in central Colorado. Maggie's older brother, Daniel, had also moved to Leadville and had found work mining silver ore. Mary Ann encouraged Maggie to come to Leadville too.

It didn't take much prodding. Maggie liked adventure. In 1886 she boarded a train to Leadville, a western boomtown nicknamed "the Greatest Mining Camp in the World." The bustling town was full of activity. New settlers arrived daily from all over the world, hoping to make their fortune.

While men could seek their fortune (or at least regular work) in the silver mines, women were not even allowed inside the mines. Instead, women worked as laundresses, teachers, cooks, nurses, and store clerks. Some women ran boardinghouses, while others made a living as "saloon girls" (prostitutes) in one of Leadville's many taverns.

When Maggie first arrived in Leadville, she lived with and kept house for her brother Daniel, who

Sources claimed that this mine in Leadville, Colorado, named "Little Johnny," was the "world's richest gold mine."

labored in a mine each day for little pay. But she soon grew bored at home and decided to look for work herself. She landed a job at Daniels, Fisher & Smith, a dry goods store on Harrison Avenue, Leadville's main drag. There Maggie sewed draperies and carpets. Her coworkers liked her. She was intelligent, charming, and fun to talk to.

Before long nineteen-year-old Margaret met someone special at a Catholic church picnic. James "J. J." Brown was a tall, handsome Irishman thirteen years older than Maggie. J. J. worked as a foreman in a silver mine. When he proposed, Maggie wasn't sure if she should accept. She had hoped to marry a wealthy man. That way, she thought, she could improve her position in life and give her parents a better home full of comforts.

"I wanted a rich man," she said, "but I loved Jim Brown."

On September 1, 1886, in Leadville's Annunciation Church, Maggie and J. J. were married. Within the next few years, Maggie's parents and siblings were all living in Leadville.

Both J. J. and Maggie wished to further their education. After their marriage, they took lessons with a tutor in Leadville. Maggie studied literature and music. She also took piano and voice lessons.

On August 30, 1887, Margaret gave birth to her first child, Lawrence Palmer Brown. A second child, Catherine Ellen, was born on July 1, 1889.

By 1892 J. J. had advanced his position at the mine. He worked as an engineer, and he became a minor stockholder in the Ibex Mining Company, a group of silver mines. A year later, one of the Ibex properties struck gold. Instantly, J. J. was a millionaire.

With newfound financial freedom, the Brown family went on a road trip to visit friends and family around the country. In Chicago they attended the Columbian Exposition of 1893, a fair exhibiting cutting-edge conveniences such as electric kitchen appliances and new products like Juicy Fruit gum, Shredded Wheat cereal, and Aunt Jemima Pancake Mix. New inventions were on display too, including George Ferris's "bicycle wheel in the sky"—the Ferris wheel.

After returning home, the Browns decided to leave Leadville for good. The family packed up their belongings and moved to Denver in 1894. After living and working for many years in the rough-hewn pioneer town, Maggie had seen her get-rich dreams become a reality. Now she set her sights on a different prize—to be accepted in the high society of Denver.

A year earlier, in 1893, Colorado women had won the right to vote in national elections, thanks to the efforts of women's suffrage leader Carrie Chapman Catt. Maggie, outgoing and strong-minded, had always been interested in public service and education. She joined several women's political clubs in the Denver area, such as the Denver Woman's Press Club, working to gain the right to vote for all women in the United

States. In 1898 she was elected chair of the Art and Literature Committee of the Denver Women's Club.

She enjoyed her role in politics, and she especially liked being part of Denver's elite women's clubs. She also liked seeing her name mentioned in the local newspapers. Many people in Denver appreciated Maggie's lively personality. "Mrs. Brown's vivacity and merry disposition is a most refreshing trait in a society woman of her position," wrote the *Denver Times,* "for in the smart set any disposition to be natural and animated is quite frowned upon."

J. J. was happy in Denver too. He enjoyed his new position as manager of his own mining company. Despite the Browns' outward success, however, they had problems in their personal life. The couple was growing more and more incompatible. Maggie flourished in the social life of Denver, while J. J. was more comfortable in his earthy mining career. Maggie shocked the community (as well as her family) when she separated from her husband in August 1909. In the early 1900s, divorce was not common.

In April 1912, aboard the *Titanic,* Maggie Brown continued to do things her own way. For one thing, she was traveling alone, which a proper lady of Maggie's day wasn't supposed to do. A lady was expected to be accompanied by a gentleman. But Maggie didn't care what people thought.

She was one of more than twenty-two hundred passengers aboard the grand ship on its very first voyage.

"But my money and jewelry!" cried the woman. "I haven't even locked the door!"

Maggie tried to reassure her. "It's only a precaution, dear," she said, convincing the woman to board the lifeboat. Maggie figured that the crew would soon repair the damage and they could all return to their cabins. A few moments later, two crewmen insisted that Maggie climb into the lifeboat too.

Twenty-three passengers sat in lifeboat No. 6 with Maggie. They included two crewmen who were aboard to captain the boat, lookout Frederick Fleet and quartermaster Robert Hichens.

Together the men slowly rowed away from the *Titanic*. In the distance, far away on the horizon, they could see a glowing light. Lifeboat No. 6 was the first to leave the *Titanic*. Soon after the lifeboat left, Captain Smith yelled for it to come back for more people. The boat held only twenty-four passengers, though it had room for sixty-five. But Hichens refused to turn around. Maggie and others encouraged him to turn back, but he told them to be quiet.

There was a real danger that when the *Titanic* sank, its suction effect would drag the surrounding vessels underwater. With only two men rowing, the lifeboat was moving very slowly. Maggie didn't see why the women on the boat couldn't help. She placed an oar in the oarlock and asked Margaret Martin, a cashier from the ship's restaurant, to hold it while she secured the other oar. The two women braced their feet on the floor of the boat and rowed hard. The lifeboat began to move faster.

The lifeboat passengers were frightened and cold. Hichens was certain that they were doomed, and he shared his worries with the other passengers. He said that their lifeboat wouldn't be found and that they would all surely freeze to death or drown. Finally Maggie put a stop to his grim predictions.

"Keep it to yourself if you feel that way!" she demanded. "We have a smooth sea and a fighting chance!"

Maggie tried to be brave, especially when she heard a great rumbling sound coming from the *Titanic*. She turned around to look back at the ship. One half of it jutted up in the air, and the ship was sinking fast.

As the ship went down, the passengers in lifeboat No. 6 sat and stared, their eyes wide with horror. Each of them had a loved one or a friend still on the doomed ship. Maggie was frightened and sad, but she wasn't ready to give up hope. Though her hands were bleeding from the vigorous rowing, she rowed harder. She encouraged others on the boat to row, telling them it would keep them warm. Maggie noticed that one man from nearby lifeboat No. 16 was wearing only pajamas. She took off one of her fur stoles and wrapped it around his legs. The two boats, tied together, floated for about an hour. Later Maggie was credited with keeping the lifeboat passengers from freezing to death.

Maggie presents a silver cup to Captain Arthur Rostron and the crew of the Carpathia *to honor their efforts in the rescue of* Titanic *survivors.*

A couple hours later, a ship came into view. Maggie was happy—they would be rescued! At about 6:00 A.M., lifeboat No. 6 arrived at the *Carpathia*, the ship that was waiting to rescue them. It took nearly five hours for the lifeboat passengers to be rescued. When the twenty lifeboats arrived at the rescue ship, most of the survivors were so cold and tired that they needed help getting aboard. About 20 percent of the people who were on the *Titanic* lifeboats later died of exposure to the cold. About 1,600 people from the ship drowned, including most of the third-class passengers. But everyone aboard lifeboat No. 6 lived, helped by the brave actions and clear thinking of Margaret Tobin Brown.

Maggie's efforts to help her fellow passengers didn't stop when survivors reached the safety of the *Carpathia*. Many survivors had lost loved ones in the tragedy. Others had lost money and possessions. Maggie herself lost thousands of dollars' worth of jewelry. Before the *Carpathia* reached New York, Maggie had helped form the Survivors Committee and raised nearly ten thousand dollars for survivors and their families.

On May 29, 1912, Maggie, as chair of the Survivors Committee, presented a silver cup to Captain Arthur Rostron of the *Carpathia*. She also presented a medal to each crew member.

Maggie Brown continued her political and humanitarian work throughout her life. In 1914 she ran for the U.S. Senate—eight years before women had the right to vote. Although she didn't win the election, she was one of the first women in the United States to run for political office.

In 1914 Maggie helped organize an international women's rights conference in Newport, Rhode Island. During World War I, Maggie worked with the American Committee for Devastated France, helping American and French soldiers. In 1932 Maggie was awarded the French Legion of Honor for her "overall good citizenship."

Margaret Tobin Brown died of a brain tumor on October 26, 1932, in New York. Her estranged husband, J. J. Brown, had died ten years earlier. Margaret was buried next to J. J. on Long Island, New York.

Calamity Jane seemed to enjoy her celebrity status in the Wild West.

Chapter **FOUR**

THE WILDEST WEST: FEMALE OUTLAWS AND REBELS

CALAMITY JANE: MARTHA JANE CANNARY

(1852–1903)

This time Calamity Jane had gone too far. And the proper ladies of Deadwood, Dakota Territory, intended to do something about it. Not only did Calamity dress like a man and drink too much and get in fights—now she was working as a bartender in a saloon! A woman, they thought, had no business in a bar, drinking and cavorting with men. A lady belonged in the home, caring for her family. And if she was single, like Calamity, she ought to make an honest living as a schoolteacher or a seamstress.

The women of Deadwood saw it as their duty to reform Calamity, which included taking a scissors to her stringy hair. No decent woman wore her hair down, unwashed and unkempt, they believed.

"They came into the saloon with a horse whip and shears to cut my hair," recalled Calamity. But Calamity wouldn't stand for any of their nonsense. "I jumped off the bar into their midst and before they could say sickem I had them [running]!"

Reportedly, fearing for their lives, the townswomen never bothered Calamity again.

Who was Calamity Jane? She was a legendary character of both fiction and real life. She was the brave heroine of Wild West novels and an adventurer in the Black Hills of South Dakota. She was tall and muscular, and she carried a gun in a holster on her hip. She swore, chewed tobacco, and drank heavily. Her face was weathered, dark, and lined from spending many years outdoors without the protection of a sunbonnet. She always looked older than she really was.

Written accounts of Calamity's life differ. It's hard to determine what is true, mainly because she liked making up stories about herself, some of which she recounted in her autobiography. Fiction writers also came up with stories about Calamity in western novels.

This much is certain—Calamity Jane lived her life boldly and did as she pleased. And she didn't let many people get close to her.

"I do not know much about her early life—I guess nobody else does but herself," said entertainer Buffalo Bill, who had known her for many years.

According to her own account, Calamity Jane was born as Martha Jane Cannary on May 1, 1852, in Princeton, Missouri. Her father, Robert, and her mother, Charlotte, were natives of Ohio. Martha was their first child. Later she had two brothers and three sisters. Unlike most girls of her day, who were interested in homemaking skills like cooking and sewing, Martha preferred to spend time outdoors with her father and brothers.

"As a child I always had a fondness for adventure and outdoor exercise," she wrote in her autobiography. She especially loved to ride horses. "I began to ride at an early age and continued to do so until I became an expert rider being able to ride the most vicious and stubborn of horses, in fact the greater portion of my life in early times was spent in this manner."

In 1865 Martha's parents announced their plan to leave Missouri and head farther west, to Virginia City, Montana. Like many families who migrated west, they hoped for a more prosperous life in the newer settlements. Traveling by covered wagon, the family met with many difficulties along the way. But thirteen-year-old Martha enjoyed the adventure. She liked being able to ride her pony every day, and the men taught her to shoot and hunt.

Later Calamity Jane recalled her travels west in her autobiography. "While on the way the greater portion of my time was spent in hunting along with the men and hunters of the party, in fact I was at all times with the men when there was excitement and adventures to be had."

In 1866, five months after leaving their home in Missouri, the Cannarys finally reached Virginia City, according to Martha. Shortly after their arrival, in the spring of 1867, the family left Montana in search of better opportunities in Utah. On the way there, in Blackfoot, Montana, Martha's mother became ill and died. The rest of the family arrived in Salt Lake City, Utah, in the summer. Soon afterward Martha's father became sick. Like his wife, he died from a sudden illness. The Cannary children had no choice but to try to make it on their own. They continued their journey, and in May 1868, they arrived in Fort Bridger, Wyoming. Martha hunted for food and took odd jobs to help support her brothers and sisters.

According to Calamity Jane's autobiography, she had become an excellent rider and markswoman, and she figured she could put her skills to good use. U.S. Cavalry Colonel George Armstrong Custer needed scouts in his campaign to fight the Sioux, Cheyenne, and other Indians on the Great Plains.

"When I joined Custer I donned the uniform of a soldier," wrote Calamity Jane. "It was a bit awkward at first but I soon got to be perfectly at home in men's clothes."

According to Calamity Jane's autobiography, she earned her famous nickname on one of her missions

As a scout for Colonel George Armstrong Custer's cavalry, Martha felt right at home in the saddle.

for the army in 1873. At Goose Creek, Wyoming, under the command of a Captain Egan, Martha Jane and her fellow soldiers were heading back to their military camp one day when they were ambushed by a large group of Sioux Indians. Captain Egan was shot and started to fall from his horse. Martha Jane circled back. With great effort, she pulled Captain Egan onto her horse and rode him safely back to the army camp. When the captain recovered from his injuries, he said to Martha Jane, "I name you Calamity Jane, the heroine of the plains."

Most historians do not believe Calamity Jane's account of how she got her nickname. Biographer J. Leonard Jennewein wrote, "There is no authenticated version of how Calamity acquired the name 'Calamity.' The story as given in her autobiography is known to be false. All we can say is that she lived in an adventurous time and place and that someone tagged her with the name 'Calamity' and it stuck."

In the 1870s, Calamity Jane worked in the Black Hills of South Dakota, protecting gold and silver miners and settlers from Indian attack. She also worked as a message dispatcher between U.S. Cavalry camps. Her duties included swimming across a large river to deliver important messages and then riding—wet and cold—ninety miles on her horse.

Calamity didn't like to stay anywhere for long. She soon headed for Fort Laramie, where she met the legendary Western scout William Hickok, better known as Wild Bill Hickok. The two traveled together to Deadwood, Dakota Territory, arriving in June 1876. Later Calamity claimed that she and Wild Bill had a romance, but this may have been one of her tall tales.

Wild Bill Hickok

A scene from Lower Main Street in Deadwood, Dakota Territory, in 1877

Hickok said that he and Calamity Jane were never anything but casual acquaintances.

While Calamity was often rowdy and wild, she had a kind and generous side too. Many people in Deadwood had good things to say about Calamity. "She was outstanding, that woman was ... if she had a chance to [help] somebody ... out of a tight place she was right there," remembered Charles Haas, who knew Calamity. "Lots of us ... knew the better side of Calamity. But then, you know, she would go to these bawdy houses and dance halls and it was 'whoopee' and soon she was drunk and then, well, things just sort of went haywire with old Calamity!"

On August 2, 1876, Wild Bill Hickok was playing poker in a saloon in Deadwood when he was shot in the back of the head by outlaw Jack McCall. When he was killed, Hickok was holding aces and eights in his hand—a grouping that was thereafter called "the dead man's hand."

Calamity claimed to have gone after Jack McCall with a meat cleaver when she heard the news. But the story wasn't substantiated.

Although it is difficult to separate truth from fiction when it comes to Calamity Jane, it is known that she acted heroically on at least one occasion. In 1876 a smallpox epidemic swept through Deadwood. The disease, which had no cure, was highly contagious. Hundreds of people became ill, and most citizens were afraid to help the victims. Dr. Babcock, the town's only physician, remembered how Calamity risked her life to care for dying miners. He also recalled that she cared for a young boy named Charles Robinson, who recovered because of her attention.

Calamity left Deadwood in the fall of 1877. Over the next few years, she prospected for gold, drove mule trains, and for a while, owned a cattle ranch in Yellowstone. All the while, she continued to drink heavily.

In 1884 she went to Texas. In El Paso, thirty-two-year-old Calamity met Clinton Burk, a native of Texas, whom she married in August 1885. "I thought I had travelled through life long enough alone and thought it was about time to take a partner for the rest of my days," Calamity wrote in her autobiography. As with many aspects of her life, however, this marriage is questioned by some historians.

Calamity and Clinton remained in Texas until 1889, when they moved to Boulder, Colorado. There, they kept a hotel for a few years. In the fall of 1895, Calamity returned to Deadwood with her husband.

Calamity Jane had been away for many years, but the people of Deadwood had not forgotten her. She had become a legend in the town's history, the daring "woman scout" of the Black Hills. Calamity enjoyed the attention, and she earned a few dollars selling copies of her life story. Promoters from the East Coast, traveling through Deadwood, encouraged Calamity Jane to appear in Wild West shows in eastern cities.

Calamity enjoyed her status as a western celebrity, though critics slammed her shows. In reality the "famous female scout of the Wild West," the "Heroine of a Thousand Thrilling Adventures," had become a worn-down, ailing alcoholic.

Indeed, Calamity's years of heavy drinking had taken their toll on her health. In July 1903, she became ill. On August 1, Calamity died at the age of fifty-one. Her undertaker was Charles Robinson, whom she had nursed back to health during the Deadwood smallpox epidemic.

John Sohn, a longtime Deadwood shoemaker, described Calamity's funeral: "There was an awful lot of people in [the funeral parlor]. I seen the picture they took; they had her propped up kinda, in a sitting position. She looked purty good, Old Calamity did."

Not everyone who visited Calamity in the funeral parlor had good intentions. Some townswomen brought in scissors and clipped locks of her hair. An old acquaintance of Calamity's put a stop to that by building a wire screen around her body.

On the day of Calamity's funeral, people traveled from distant towns to pay their respects to the Black Hills legend. And the townspeople of Deadwood showed their respect for the wild-natured frontier woman. They granted Calamity Jane her dying wish and buried her next to her hero, Wild Bill Hickok.

Calamity Jane tips her hat in front of Wild Bill Hickok's grave, where she would later be buried.

Infamous stagecoach robber Pearl Hart, on left.

A PEARL IN THE ROUGH: PEARL HART

(1871–1960)

Pearl Hart could make a claim that no other woman—or man—could. She was the first known stagecoach robber in Arizona Territory.

Pearl Hart was born in 1871 in Ontario, Canada. She ran away from home when she was seventeen and ended up in Arizona. From that point on, Pearl was trouble.

In 1889 she met a miner named Joe Boot. Together the couple embarked on a life of crime, working as a team. Pearl first lured men to her room, promising them romance. But once the men were in her room, Joe knocked them out and took their money.

For more excitement and financial gain, Pearl and Joe decided to rob stagecoaches. To disguise her identity, Pearl cut her hair and wore men's clothing. But Pearl and Joe weren't clever thieves. After they robbed a Globe, Arizona, stagecoach of $400, they took off on their horses—and got lost.

The next morning, the sheriff found them asleep beneath some trees. Pearl was arrested and put on trial. Luckily for her, she was a convincing actress. She told the jury that she had robbed the stagecoach because her mother in Canada was ill and needed the money. The jury believed her. Pearl was released, only to be arrested again a short time later for unlawfully carrying a gun.

Pearl was sent to the Yuma Territorial Prison in Arizona. Not only was she the first woman to be sent to the prison, she was also the only prisoner to become pregnant while confined there. The scandal served Pearl well. The only two men who had been alone with her in her cell were the governor of Arizona and a Christian minister. Pearl was released.

In her later years, Pearl performed as a stagecoach-robbing outlaw for a short time with Buffalo Bill's Wild West show. Eventually she returned to Arizona, where she married a rancher and lived a crime-free life.

CHARLEY PARKHURST

harley Parkhurst drove a stagecoach for the California Stage Lines in the 1850s. Charley had a pleasant disposition. He also had a scarred face, a dislocated cheekbone, and a missing eye. He dressed in dirty, oversized trousers, and he liked to smoke and chew tobacco.

On December 19, 1879, the day Charley died, his true identity was revealed—Charley Parkhurst was a woman! A local newspaper wrote, "It could scarcely be believed by persons who knew Charley Parkhurst for a quarter of a century." Charley had been born Charlotte Parkhurst. After Charlotte was placed in an orphanage at an early age, she put on boys' clothes and ran away. From then on, she presented herself to the world as Charley.

THE WILDCATS:
CATTLE ANNIE AND LITTLE BRITCHES

Annie McDougall and Jennie Stevens stood back and admired the handsome, wild-natured cowboys kicking up their heels at an 1894 Guthrie, Oklahoma, dance. "Know who they are?" asked a friend. When the teenage girls shook their heads, he said, "That's Bill Doolin and some of his boys."

The Doolin gang—Red Buck, Charley Pierce, and Bill Doolin—were known for their daring exploits. The boys looked wild and dangerous, and they impressed

Cattle Annie, left, *and Little Britches,* right, *were young outlaws who made their mark on the Wild West.*

Annie, who was seventeen, and Jennie, sixteen. That night the girls made a pact. They would run away from home and become famous outlaws with the Doolin boys.

The gang hired the teens as lookouts, and soon the young women were known as "Cattle Annie" and "Little Britches." When the Doolin gang broke up, the girls made their way the best they could. They sold whiskey to the Osage Indians and stole cattle. Wanted for several crimes, they were eventually captured by U.S. marshals at a farmhouse near Pawnee, Oklahoma.

Cattle Annie and Little Britches were shipped to a prison in Boston. On the East Coast, they became celebrities. Crowds formed outside the prison, hoping to catch a glimpse of the "Oklahoma Girl Bandits" on the prison grounds. After serving two years in prison, however, Annie and Jennie didn't think the outlaw life seemed so glamorous anymore. Annie married and settled down near Pawnee. Jennie moved to New York to find work. Two years later, she died of tuberculosis.

THE BANDIT QUEEN: BELLE STARR (MYRA BELLE SHIRLEY)

(1849–1889)

Though she was raised to be "ladylike" by her aristo-cratic, wealthy parents, Belle Starr was born to be a rebel. Although she had big brown eyes and dark hair,

Despite her long gowns, the notorious Belle Starr was a force to reckon with.

Belle was described as "hatchet-faced" and mean as a rattlesnake. She liked to drink and swear.

When she was eighteen, living with her parents in Scyne, Texas, Belle met an attractive, dangerous man named Cole Younger. He was an outlaw and a close friend of the notorious bank robber Jesse James. Belle was smitten. She ran off with Younger and joined his outlaw gang.

A few months later, Belle returned home. She was pregnant. In 1867 her daughter, Pearl Younger, was born. Belle nicknamed the little girl Rosie.

Belle didn't stay single for long. At age twenty, she met James Reed. Her parents approved of the match at first. They liked the fact that Reed had been a Confederate soldier in the Civil War, fighting for the Southern states. But Reed was an outlaw too, and like Younger, he was a friend of the James brothers.

Belle married Jim Reed in 1868, and they soon had a son, Ed. While Belle adored her children, she liked living wildly a bit more. She wasn't called "the Bandit Queen" for nothing. Usually disguised as a man, Belle robbed several stagecoaches and banks throughout the West. She especially liked to steal horses. Although she was arrested for her crimes many times, she always managed to wiggle her way out of trouble with her charm. She was sent to jail once, but after seducing her captor, she was released.

Belle liked stealing and making trouble, and she loved men. Throughout her life she had many lovers.

Belle usually didn't stay with any man for very long. She was known for using her lovers to get what she wanted.

In 1880 Belle married Sam Starr, a wild-natured Cherokee. Belle and Sam Starr settled on Sam's thousand acres of tribal land along the Canadian River in Oklahoma, calling the place "Younger's Bend" in honor of Belle's first love, Cole Younger.

Belle lived happily on her land with her family— Sam, Pearl, then thirteen, and Ed, who was about ten.

Belle rides with her husband Sam Starr, right, *who was wanted for thievery at the time of his death by both the U.S. government and Cherokee tribal leaders.*

She greatly enjoyed her privacy—she didn't miss the company of other women a bit. "So long have I been estranged from the society of women (whom I thoroughly detest), that I thought it would be irksome to be in their midst," Belle told a newspaper reporter in 1889.

Though she liked her homestead, Belle wasn't quite ready to settle down. In 1883 Belle and Sam were arrested for horse theft. Newspapers nationwide carried news of the event, and Belle was nicknamed "The Petticoat Terror of the Plains." During Belle's trial, her children were sent to live with friends. Belle and Sam were sentenced to nine months in jail. Belle, true to form, became friends with the warden and his wife. She had an easy, pleasant time in jail and was released early. Sam, on the other hand, served his full sentence, working at heavy labor.

Belle wasn't ready to mend her ways. When Sam was released from jail, the pair joined a gang of horse thieves. Belle, always the dominant one in a group, was the "queen" of the gang. In 1886, when Belle was thirty-eight, Sam Starr was killed during an argument at a friend's party.

When Sam died, Belle worried that she would lose her home on Cherokee land. In a sly move, she married another Cherokee, Jim July, a handsome, well-educated man of twenty-four. According to tribal law, Belle and her new husband could stay on the land at Younger's Bend.

Belle Starr's tombstone reads:
Shed not for her the bitter tear,
Nor give the heart to vain regret.
'Tis but the casket that lies here,
The gem that filled it sparkles yet.

Belle had made too much trouble in her life not to have enemies. On February 3, 1889, at age forty-one, she was riding her horse near her home when she was shot, first in the face and then in the back. She fell from her horse, dead.

Two days later, the Fort Smith *Elevator* carried the headline, "BELLE STARR MURDERED FROM AMBUSH BY UNKNOWN PARTIES." No one ever discovered who killed her.

Many stories about the Wild West embellish the truth about those who dared to live there.

Chapter **FIVE**

THE WEST OF FACT AND FICTION

IMAGES OF THE **WILD WEST** ARE A MAINSTAY OF American culture—tough-talking cowboys and cowgirls, rowdy saloon brawls, and good guys fighting outlaws. Novels, television shows, movies, and plays have told many stories about the West—and many myths. The West as it is popularly understood is largely a product of people's imaginations. And people continue to be fascinated with the West of fact *and* fiction.

Why did the American West become mythologized? From the start, U.S. citizens loved the idea of the frontier, seeing it as a paradise that held endless possibilities. In hard economic times, the prospect of a better life in the West gave people hope.

REEXAMINING THE PAST

ver time writers and historians have examined the American West with a new awareness of the myths that have existed since the beginning of U.S. history. For instance, East Coast hopefuls traveled the overland trails in the 1800s in search of the promised "paradise." But many of these travelers were disappointed to find a harsh environment and endless toil. The move west split up families and left many women and men isolated and lonely.

Racism was another widespread problem in the old West. The U.S. government robbed the Native American people of their homelands and relocated them to reservations. Chinese Americans were denied basic civil rights in the West. In the late 1800s, the California Constitution read, "No native of China . . . shall ever exercise the privileges of an elector [the right to vote]."

That idea has not changed since the days of the western frontier. People still hope and work for better lives for themselves and their families. Many people like to learn about brave heros and heroines who fought for what they believed. The strong-willed free spirits of the Wild West are inspiring.

Even while Calamity Jane and Wild Bill Hickok were alive, readers could buy dime novels about these well-known western "characters." Typically their exploits were exaggerated and sometimes made up entirely. Calamity Jane had a healthy ego and liked her fame.

She often boasted about her adventures, which usually involved stretching the truth a bit. Historians agree that much of Martha Cannary's autobiography, *Calamity Jane, Written by Herself,* is fiction.

Because book and theater audiences enjoy action and drama, authors who wrote about women like Calamity Jane, Annie Oakley, and Maggie Brown often glamorized them or embellished the facts to make a better story. In turn, folk legends were born.

Gifted sharpshooter Annie Oakley was a star during her lifetime, but she became larger than life after her death. Her life has been depicted in books, plays, and films, most notably in composer Irving Berlin's popular musical, *Annie Get Your Gun.*

More dramatized stories of the West came with the invention of television. In the 1950s, more than thirty western-themed TV shows were on the air, featuring cowboy actors such as Gene Autry and Roy Rogers. A comedy show called *Annie Oakley and Tagg* featured the partly fictionalized antics of Annie Oakley. Western-themed TV shows and films are still very popular.

Perhaps no Western woman has been the subject of more wild fictionalizing than Margaret Tobin Brown. In the 1930s, *Denver Post* writer Gene Fowler wrote a colorful account of her life in a chapter of his novel, *Timberline.* In the book, Maggie is portrayed as a crude, cussing, pistol-packing eccentric. Fowler made up details, such as how she once hid (and accidentally burned) the family's savings in a potbellied stove.

Her actions aboard *Titanic*'s lifeboat No. 6 also came from Fowler's imagination, including a tale about how she stripped down to her corset and bloomers, selflessly giving her wool clothing and fur wraps (including her "sixty-thousand-dollar chinchilla opera cloak") to shivering children and frail older women. Romance novelist Carolyn Bancroft wrote an equally vivid account in a 1930s magazine article, which was turned into a popular booklet called *The Unsinkable Mrs. Brown.*

Brown biographer Kristen Iversen wrote, "These fantastic stories fed an eager public and played into

Society woman Maggie Brown didn't bother to correct half-truths that circulated about her, including stories that later contributed to the fictionalized portrayal of her life onstage.

well-established stereotypes of unconventional women—and no one bothered to check the facts."

Later Bancroft's story served as the basis for the 1960 Broadway musical, *The Unsinkable Molly Brown*. Playwright Richard Morris said he used the name "Molly" because it was easier to sing. Not only were most of the facts about "Molly" Brown made up in this play, but her name was also an invention. Margaret Brown was never called Molly in her life!

This misnomer was perpetuated with the 1964 movie *The Unsinkable Molly Brown*, starring Debbie Reynolds. And Margaret Brown continues to be misrepresented. In James Cameron's acclaimed 1997 film *Titanic*, Margaret (once again called Molly) is portrayed as a bawdy social misfit. In reality Maggie was an opinionated but popular society woman.

Although the made-up facts about Margaret Brown's life are interesting and fun, her real-life actions were no less amazing. Throughout her life, she campaigned for human rights. At a time when women were expected to accept their position as nonvoting, second-class citizens, she fought for women's right to vote, and she campaigned to become a U.S. senator. She also supported the temperance movement—a social movement, led mainly by women, to outlaw alcohol—because she wanted to help women who were abused by alcoholic husbands.

"Most women in 1912 did not travel without husbands or male escorts and would hardly have stood

Cattle women brand cattle at a ranch in San Luis Valley, Colorado. Although they were less well known, thousands of women were part of the American frontier.

up to a male authority figure as [she did] in the lifeboat," said Margaret Brown's great-granddaughter, Muffet Brown.

Brown and other pioneering women challenged traditional ideas about women's roles. Annie Oakley, for instance, proved that a woman could excel at an activity typically associated with men—shooting a gun. "Her spunky independence and her amazing accomplishments [foretold] a future in which women would emerge from . . . narrow notions of roles and respectability, [that] imprisoned them in absurd clothes, and kept their hair up and their options down," wrote one historian.

Western women showed that a woman's place was not just in the home—she could also be pushing a plow in the field, selling real estate, or working as a doctor, stagecoach driver, or politician. Notable women throughout the West made "firsts" for women everywhere. In 1869 Esther Morris helped win the right to vote for women in Wyoming, long before women elsewhere in the country gained suffrage. Ex-slave Clara Brown traveled to Colorado and became a successful businesswoman. She also established the first Sunday school in Denver.

Calamity Jane, Charley Parkhurst, and Pearl Hart bucked tradition entirely and laughed in the face of sexual stereotypes. Other western travelers, such as Laura Ingalls Wilder, and Virginia Reed—as well as countless others—made a difference in quieter but no less powerful ways. Bravely and often unknowingly, the women of the Wild West played a meaningful role in a swiftly changing time.

SOURCES

7–8   J. Leonard Jennewein, *Calamity Jane of the Western Trails* (Huron, SD: Huron Books, 1953), 32.

14   JoAnn Levy, *They Saw the Elephant: Women in the California Goldrush,* n.d., <www.goldrush.com/~joann/women.htm>.

15   Ibid.

16   Paula Bartley and Cathy Loxton, *Plainswomen: Women in the American West* (New York: Cambridge University Press, 1991), 45.

21   Virginia R. Murphy, "Across the Plains in the Donner Party," *Century* XLII, 1891, 411.

22   Dee Brown, *The Gentle Tamers: Women of the Old West* (Lincoln, NE: University of Nebraska Press, 1958), 96.

26   Ibid., 99.

26–27   The Lockley Files, Oregon Collection at the University of Oregon Library, Eugene, Oregon.

28   Elliott West, "Family Life on the Trail of the West," *History Today,* December 1992, 33.

29   Susan Shelby Magoffin, *Down the Santa Fe Trail and into Mexico* (New Haven, CT: Yale University Press, 1926), 4.

30   Oregon Pioneer Association, 19th Annual Reunion, Transaction (Portland, OR: Oregon Pioneer Association, 1891), 42.

31   The Lockley Files, University of Oregon.

32   Nancy Wilson Ross, *Westward the Women* (San Francisco: North Point Press, 1985), 16.

32–33   Roger Welsch, "A Song for the Pioneers," *Audubon,* November–December 1992, 112.

33   The Lockley Files, University of Oregon.

33   Laura Ingalls Wilder, *Little House on the Prairie* (New York: Harper and Row, 1935), 1.

35   Wilder, *Little House,* 212, 213.

37   Laura Ingalls Wilder, *On the Banks of Plum Creek* (New York: Harper and Row, 1937), 194.

43   Jennifer Slegg, "Fan Letter Reply by Laura Ingalls Wilder," My Little House on the Prairie Home Page, n.d., <www.pinc.com/%7Ejenslegg/misclett.htm>.

45   Nancy Schimmel, "Little Sure Shot," words and music
     © 1980 by Nancy Schimmel. Used by permission. For
     more information, write to Sisters' Choice Recording
     and Books/704 Gilman/Berkeley, CA 94710.

46   Damaine Vonada, "Annie Oakley Was More Than a 'Crack
     Shot in Petticoats,'" *Smithsonian*, September 1990, 131.

47–48 Glenda Riley, *The Life and Legacy of Annie Oakley*
     (Norman, OK: University of Oklahoma Press, 1994), 11.

48   Shirl Kasper, *Annie Oakley* (Norman, OK: University of
     Oklahoma Press, 1992), 6.

48   Ibid.

49   Isabelle S. Sayers, *Annie Oakley and Buffalo Bill's Wild
     West* (New York: Dover Publications, 1981), 4.

50   Riley, 12.

50   Kasper, 7.

51   Riley, 12.

52   Kasper, 16, 17.

53   Ibid.

53   Ibid.

54   Courtney Riley Cooper, *Annie Oakley: Woman at Arms*
     (New York: Duffield, 1927), 65.

58   Kasper, 22.

69   Kristen Iversen, *Unraveling the Myth: The Story of Molly
     Brown* (Boulder, CO: Johnson Publishing, 1999), 90.

71   Ibid., 147.

74   Iversen, 16.

75   Logan Marshall, *The Sinking of the* Titanic (Seattle: Hara
     Publishing, 1998), 112.

80   Joan Swallow Reiter, *The Women (The Old West;* vol. 23).
     (New York: Time-Life Books, 1978), n.p.

80   Janet Ratzloff, "Calamity Jane" Cowgal's Home on the
     Web, n.d., <www.cowgirls.com>.

81   Roberta Beed Sollid, *Calamity Jane: A Study in Historical
     Criticism* (Helena, MT: The Western Press/Historical
     Society of Montana, 1958), 125.

81–82 Ibid., 125.

82   Ibid., 126.

83   Ibid., 127.

83   Jennewein, 32.

85   Ibid., 33.

86–87   Ibid., 38.

87–88   Ibid., 33.

   91   Floyd D. P. Øydegaard, "She Was a Man!" Shadows of the Past, Inc., n.d., <www.sptddog.com/sotp/parkhurst. html>.

   91   James D. Horan and Paul Sann, *Pictorial History of the Wild West* (New York: Crown, 1954), 171.

   96   Richard Young and Judy Dockney, *Outlaw Tales: Legends, Myths, and Folklore from America's Middle Border* (Little Rock, AR: August House, 1992), 203.

   97   Ibid., 40.

  100   Miriam Horn, "How the West Was Really Won," *U.S. News and World Report,* 21 May 1990, 56.

102–103 Iversen, xv.

103–104   Muffet Brown, interview by author, 27 February 1999.

  104   Vonada, 131.

SELECTED BIBLIOGRAPHY

BOOKS

Bartley, Paula, and Cathy Loxton. *Plains Women: Women in the American West.* New York: Cambridge University Press, 1991.

Brown, Dee. *The Gentle Tamers: Women of the Old Wild West.* Lincoln, NE: University of Nebraska Press, 1958.

Iversen, Kristen. *Unraveling the Myth: The Story of Molly Brown.* Boulder, CO: Johnson Publishing, 1999.

Jameson, Elizabeth, and Susan Armitage, eds. *Writing the Range: Race, Class and Culture in the Women's West.* Norman, OK: University of Oklahoma Press, 1997.

Jennewein, J. Leonard. *Calamity Jane of the Western Trails.* Huron, SD: Dakota Books, 1953.

Kasper, Shirl. *Annie Oakley.* Norman, OK: University of Oklahoma Press, 1992.

Levy, JoAnn. *They Saw the Elephant: Women in the California Goldrush.* Hamden, CT: Archon Books, 1990.

Miller, John E. *Becoming Laura Ingalls Wilder: The Woman Behind the Legend*. Columbia, MO: University of Missouri Press, 1998.

Peavy, Linda, and Ursula Smith. *Pioneer Women: The Lives of Women on the Frontier*. New York: Smithmark Publishers, 1997.

Riley, Glenda. *The Life and Legacy of Annie Oakley*. Norman, OK: University of Oklahoma, 1994.

Seagraves, Anne. *Daughters of the West*. Hayden, ID: Wesanne Publications, 1996.

Sollid, Roberta Beed. *Calamity Jane: A Study in Historical Criticism*. Helena, MT: The Western Press/Montana Historical Society Press, 1958.

Stewart, Elinore Pruitt. *Letters of a Woman Homesteader*. Boston: Houghton Mifflin, 1982.

WEBSITES

Annie Oakley Foundation <miston.com/annieoakley/>
My Little House on the Praire Home Page
    <vvv.com/~jenslegg/index.htm>
New Light on the Donner Party
    <www.metrogourmet.com/crossroads/KJhome.htm>
New Perspectives on THE WEST <www.pbs.org/weta/thewest/>
The Oregon Trail Home page
    <www.isu.edu/~trinmich/Oregontrail.html>

INDEX

OTHER TITLES FROM LERNER AND A&E®:

Arthur Ashe

Bill Gates

Bruce Lee

Chief Crazy Horse

Christopher Reeve

George Lucas

Gloria Estefan

Jacques Cousteau

Jesse Owens

Jesse Ventura

John Glenn

Legends of Dracula

Louisa May Alcott

Madeleine Albright

Maya Angelou

Mother Teresa

Nelson Mandela

Princess Diana

Queen Cleopatra

Rosie O'Donnell

Saint Joan of Arc

Wilma Rudolph

Women in Space

ABOUT THE AUTHOR

Katherine Krohn is the author of several biographies for young readers, including *Marilyn Monroe: Norma Jeane's Dream, Elvis Presley: The King, Rosie O'Donnell,* and *Princess Diana.* Ms. Krohn is also a journalist and a fiction writer. She lives in Eugene, Oregon.

PHOTO ACKNOWLEDGMENTS

Wyoming State Museum, pp. 2, 22; Library of Congress, pp. 6, 12, 72, 83, 88; State Historical Society of North Dakota, pp. 11, 32; painting by Robert Lindneux, Woolaroc Museum, Bartlesville, OK, p. 13; Archive Photos: (Hirz) p. 14, (Archive) pp. 58, 84, 98, (American Stock) p. 78; Corbis-Bettmann, pp. 15, 64; Denver Public Library, pp. 17, 52, 56, 65, 67, 68, 76, 95, 102; The Kansas State Historical Society, Topeka, pp. 18, 28; California Department of Parks and Recreation Photographic Archives, p. 20; The Bancroft Library, University of California, Berkeley, p. 25; © LDS Church, Courtesy of the Church Historical Department. Used by permission, p. 27; Laura Ingalls Wilder Memorial Society, De Smet, SD, pp. 35, 40; Laura Ingalls Wilder Home Association, Mansfield, MO, pp. 41, 42; Solomon D. Butcher Collection/Nebraska State Historical Society, p. 36; Ohio Historical Society, pp. 44, 48; Garst Museum, Greenville, OH, pp. 55, 59; Buffalo Bill Historical Center, Cody, WY, p. 57; Circus World Museum, Baraboo, WI, p. 62; Adams Memorial Museum, Deadwood, SD, p. 85; Arizona Historical Society, Tucson, p. 89; Division of Manuscripts, University of Oklahoma Library, Rose Collection, #2127, p. 92; Western History Collections, University of Oklahoma Libraries, p. 93; Fred S. Barde Collection, Oklahoma Historical Society, #4639, p. 97; Colorado Historical Society, neg. #28,537, p. 104.

Cover photos
Hardcover: front, Colorado Historical Society, #F4715, (upper left); American Stock/Archive Photos (upper right and center); Arizona Historical Society, Tucson, (lower left); Library of Congress (lower right); back, Ohio Historical Society.
Softcover: front, Ohio Historical Society; back, Buffalo Bill Historical Center, Cody, WY.